HERMAN VIII

A HERMAN® TREASURY

by Jim Unger

Andrews and McMeel
A Universal Press Syndicate Company
Kansas City

HERMAN® is distributed internationally by Universal Press Syndicate.

Herman VIII: A Herman Treasury copyright © 1992 by Jim Unger. All rights reserved. Printed in the United States of America. No part of this book may be used or reproduced in any manner whatsoever without written permission except in the case of reprints in the context of reviews. For information write Andrews and McMeel, 4900 Main Street, Kansas City, Missouri 64112.

ISBN: 0-8362-1896-5

Library of Congress Catalog Card Number: 92-72245

I dedicate this eighth treasury collection of cartoons to all the people at Universal Press Syndicate, Andrews and McMeel, and those who work with them at home and abroad.

To my brother Bob who wrote many of the best gags and who proclaims, "I follow the herd if it happens to be going in my direction."

And to Somerset Maugham who penned, "Only mediocre people are at their best all of the time."

—JIM UNGER

Foreword

Without a shot being fired, Jim Unger is conquering the people of the world. And that's the way he likes it. "How can you not love them," he writes, "they're such poor weak creatures and every one of them reminds me of myself."

As the Berlin wall crumbled, editors in the East were quick to negotiate with Universal Press Syndicate to publish Herman in their newspapers. More recently, two books (collections of Herman cartoons) have been introduced in China.

Growing up in London, Unger says he realized he was different from an early age. His salvation came when he realized everyone else was different, too. "Whether we live in a high-rise apartment or a jungle clearing, we share the same emotions and the same excitements. We are molded by our circumstances and our religions, but we are all the same. Our imagination is our 'genius.'

"I'm just a little boy whispering to everyone that the emperor isn't wearing any clothes."

"Don't get me any more of this
roll-on deodorant."

"The doctor says your cast can come off as soon as you've paid."

"I asked you a year ago to get me some help pulling up that drawbridge."

"This hammer keeps hitting two inches to the left."

"We can't stand the sight of each other."

"Table for two. Food for five."

"We're not too happy with the caterers."

"He was laid off from the candle factory after the fire."

"Well, at least the lesson's over."

"Shall I do one for my wife while I'm here?"

"I can't find anything wrong with you.
Are you in love?"

"I can't move my head."

"Maybe it was ivory poachers."

"Don't go out during thunderstorms."

"I sent my boy to study in Florida."

"Modern technology . . . 47 floors
in six seconds."

"Are you sure?"

"Imagine you've got 12 of these babies
and a burglar breaks in."

"He's a long-haired terrier."

"I'm not absolutely sure I've got
the right suitcase."

"Are you 'Herbie's Wonder Tonic'?"

"I'll have the same as yesterday —
spaghetti and golf balls."

"I don't need to learn reading.
It's all on TV."

"That's more like it — 127 pounds."

"I lost the five grand. What's
our next step?"

"I thought it was you."

"I've decided to try shock treatment."

"If your name's on this list, they're all out."

"I'm not late. I was giving you
a little 'wait training.'"

"He had an emergency operation."

"Your cut in salary is a cost-of-living adjustment due to the falling price of coffee."

"I'll give you directions. Just don't drive above jogging speed."

"Your baggage arrived, but your wife went to Tokyo."

"We can manage on my pension. All we need is the fare to Albania."

"Looks all right to me."

"I think you've had enough. Why don't I call you a cab?"

"He doesn't need pockets."

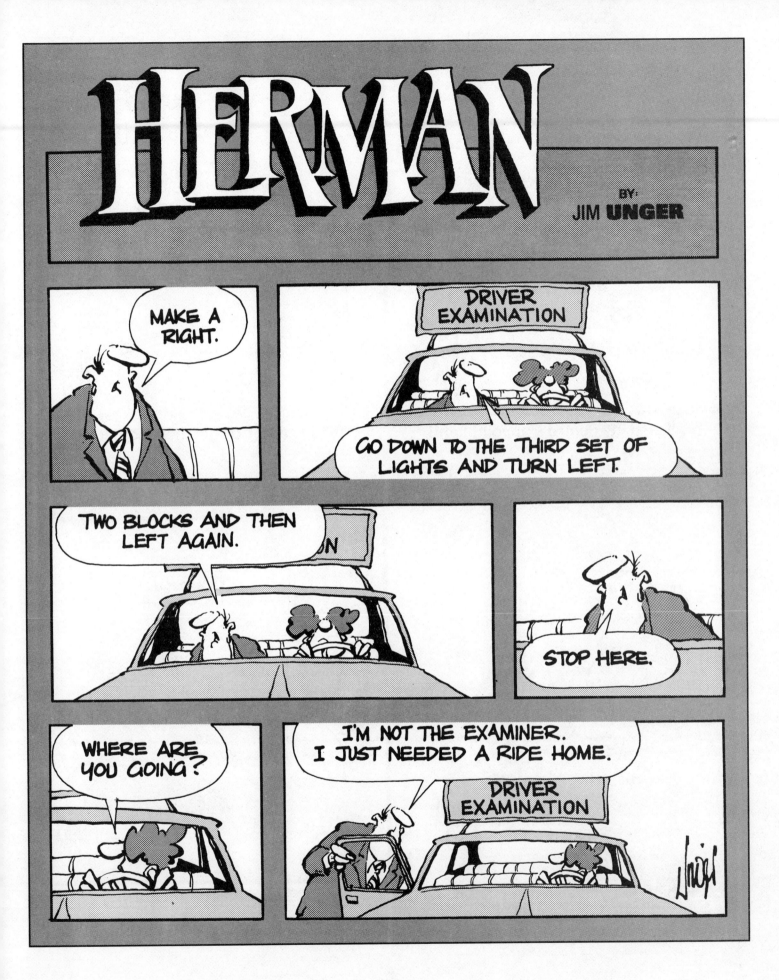

"I missed my dentist's appointment!"

"If I buy two, do I get them both free?"

"I could have left you a tip if you hadn't talked me into that cheesecake."

"Everyone at work drew straws and we lost."

"Whatever that was, I'll have another one."

"If I was a tipper, you'd definitely get one."

"I just wanted to tell you I'm gonna be late."

"Can I borrow your ashtray?"

"Give the ticket to my husband.
He taught me to drive."

"Don't get out of the car."

"Makes you wonder how we ever
managed without it."

"What have you got within
walking distance?"

"I wanna be able to breathe if I sink."

"The racetrack laundered his money again."

"Happy birthday, Ralph."

26

"We need a second car until we can afford a first one."

"Seventy-eight minutes . . . That'll be 26 bucks."

"That sign wasn't there when you went in."

"We bought you two toasters in case things don't work out."

"Is this kid yours?"

"I want to make sure nobody steps on him."

"Don't take any of these red pills, and if that doesn't work, don't take any of the blue ones."

"Can you tell me how to get to Wimpole Lane, Berry Street, Tunney Crescent, and Orchard Park Avenue?"

"It's just till I fix the hole
in our fence."

"This must be the middle of nowhere."

"What did I tell you, the guy
in the bow tie won."

"You see any rust?"

"We're still married, but we're separated."

"I can get to the supermarket
in under six minutes."

"Sixty-six flavors."

"I'll hand you over to our
washroom specialist."

"You didn't say anything on the phone
about needing a co-signer."

"We've got a prenuptial agreement. She renounces all claims for $25 cash."

"If you hadn't been hiding in the bushes, I wouldn't have been speeding."

"Your blood type is AB Inflammable."

"I'm leaving this for income tax just in case I get caught."

"They just seized a truckload of government toilet seats. The estimated street value is $2 billion."

"Are you trying to tell me that baby on the rug is not me?"

"What's a good wine to take away the taste of this food?"

"What does 86 years come out to with time off for good behavior?"

"Can I help it if your birthday coincides
with the electricity bill?"

"I knew my little girl would leave one day.
That's how I've kept my sanity."

"I think our popularity is slipping."

"She got a black belt after her first lesson."

"I wrote you love letters before we were married because I could afford stamps."

"I've decided to give you another chance. Next time case the joint first."

"When I shout 'Gun,' duck."

"I only just made it out of the last place."

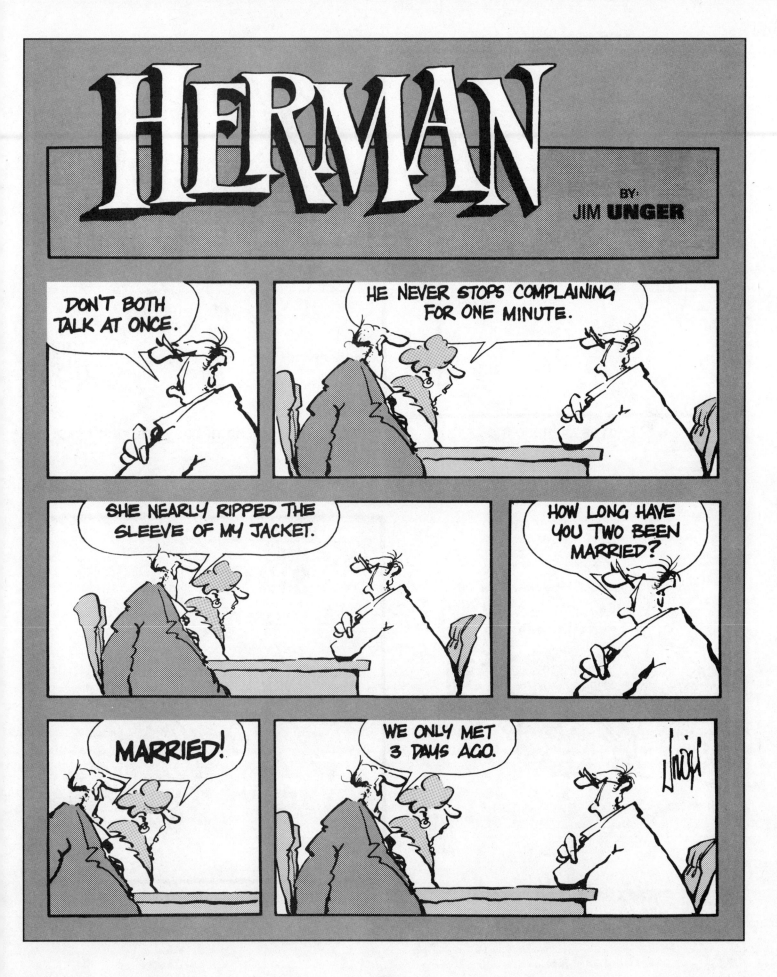

"He loves Chinese food."

"There must be somebody you don't like."

"Keep her mother happy —
wave this chicken over us."

"That suit was made for you. It's the
cheapest one we've got."

"My wife wouldn't come.
She said you're a moron."

"Where does he take the driving test?"

"He can't fix the air-conditioning if he's
carrying your luggage up the fire escape."

"One of these is a prescription and one is a
receipt from a Chinese restaurant."

"I've started my own space program. I've already thrown out her mother."

"You're going to have to stop eating on the run."

"She wants something that you don't use."

"Root canal? You've charged me for the Suez Canal."

"Keep whistling. I forgot my glasses."

"Do you want an appointment for tomorrow?"

"We've agreed on an out-of-court settlement until we can each afford a lawyer."

"Would you like a drink while they're trying to catch the catch of the day?"

"Do you seriously expect me to hurtle through the air at 30,000 feet and not smoke?"

"My money's on him."

"What's 13 hours off 65 years?"

"Your grandfather has left you his bicycle!"

"I think I've discovered why you keep grinding your teeth."

"D'you mind if I sit on that side? I'm deaf in my right ear."

"You'll need this."

"It works better than 'Stop.'"

"Pass the ketchup and one of your sausages."

"Fifty-four cents in change, a book of matches, and a bottle opener."

"Would you mind taking our picture? We forgot our camera."

" I don't want to learn to drive — I want to learn to better criticize my husband."

"If you want me to take them after meals, you'd better give me some of my $40 back."

"It's a par-12 till the groundskeeper
gets his back pay."

"Do you sell those invisible hearing aids?"

"You're gonna have to start losing weight."

"I don't know how long I've been waiting.
He's got my watch."

50

"We'll have to do another one when the fog clears."

"A whole village was without water for three days after my wife shot him."

"Put 62 cents' worth in there."

"That's 'ozone layer cake.'"

"I just asked you how the meat loaf was."

"The population of the Earth grew by 14,000 while you were searching for that nickel."

"Your last employer wants to know what you did with the canteen money."

"People couldn't spell very good in those days."

"Leave your fax number and
we'll let you know."

"Have you got anything for indigestion?"

"Any escapes today?"

"Not quite everything."

"My wife needs plenty of warning with the lemonade."

"I thought this place had a floor show."

"Are there any side effects to these pills apart from bankruptcy?"

"George is a big game hunter."

"I found wheel tracks in my roses again."

"Your flight left two hours early owing to a malfunction in the captain's watch."

"Seventy-five degrees."

"I see you're back to five meals a day."

"Can't you remember your number?"

"It's your wife. She wants a divorce."

"Alex . . . come up this end."

"He didn't say 'No,' he said 'Maybe.'"

"Chicken soup, without noodles."

"Two rolls of anything. It's for our bedroom."

"Why don't you try it out before you buy it?"

"It's Julius Caesar taking a bath."

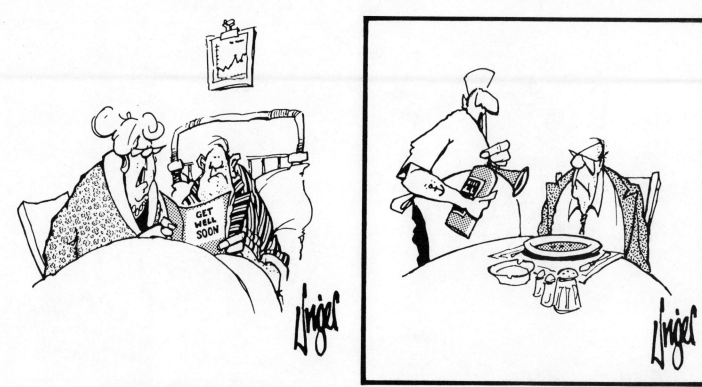

"It's from the landlord."

"You the guy with the fly in his soup?"

"That's in case you run a red light."

"Can you manage that lot in one night?"

"They only delivered to little old ladies."

"Stop burning the old guy's breakfast."

"He almost made it across the river."

"I can't hear any problems, but
that's not surprising."

"You are two completely different
personalities. That'll be
75 bucks each."

"Anyone else for the airport?"

"Dad, can I borrow the car payment?"

"The court ruled in his favor."

"I'd like to make an appointment for 8 o'clock Tuesday."

"It always speeds up when
I take my clothes off."

"These should make you relax. You won't
have any money to do anything else."

"That's your organic shampoo."

"We're nine points down. You're fired."

"We'll take the one on the left."

"Getting ready for the annual
sheep count, Mildew?"

"Taxi!"

"I see the police got your car back."

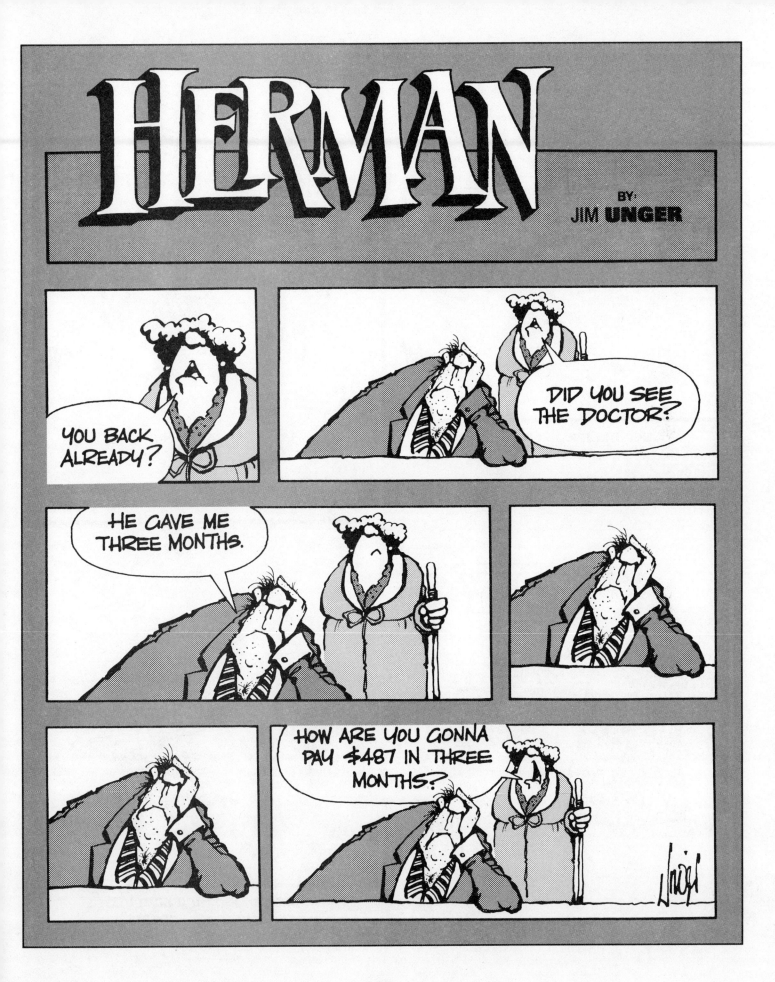

"Just imagine I'm a pizza and deliver me to my sister's."

"I decided to save you the trouble of visiting me."

X-RAY
FOLLOW THE INVISIBLE LINE

"I'm looking for a card that reflects me . . . cheap."

"I've decided to move you up the ladder. Get a bucket."

"Not much on TV."

"I hear you're not completely satisfied with your semi-private accommodation."

"It's happy hour. You get two mushroom soups."

"We get a lot of foreign visitors."

"He was the world's greatest juggler."

"Guess what 'catch of the day' is."

"I've got two chances at it this year."

"I didn't get her a birthday card.
She took the money."

"They change the beds every day!
I can never find mine!"

"The nurse says you're having
trouble getting out of bed."

"I'm a singing birthday card. Got a
piano and a couple of beers?"

"She's gonna spend my $18 tax refund on a $400 coat."

"The big ones are 15 years."

"That was $19.80, wasn't it?"

"That picture was taken when I was on the ground."

"Got a Teflon-coated frypan?"

"He's probably held up in traffic."

"That's 25 cents for the price list and
a dollar for the coffee."

"Sitting Bull's taken the saloon."

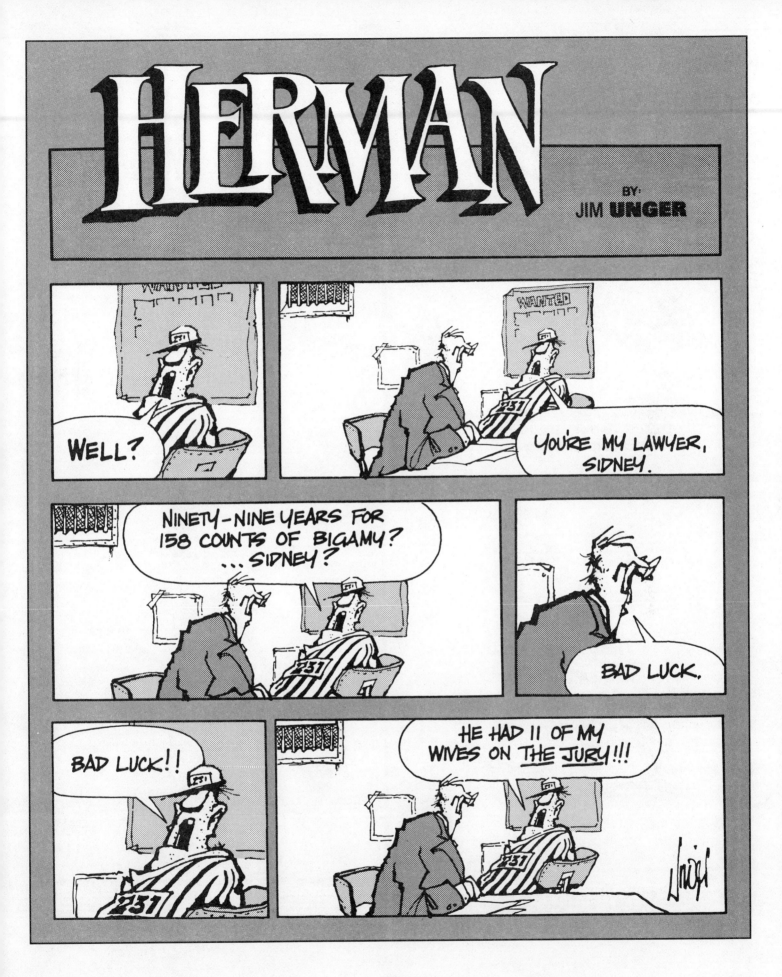

"I opened 13 dummy corporations —
now I can't find my money."

"Can you change two pieces of eight
for eight pieces of two?"

"The mirror isn't cracked; that's
the back of your head."

"Mom! . . . I'm over here."

"Tachometer for an '89 Ferrari."

"I *told* you what 'park' meant."

"I made it out of soap."

"Catch of the day from the
wine cellar, Francine."

"There's an escargot in my lettuce."

"I can't keep anything down."

"Have you ever been to Ralph's Body Shop?"

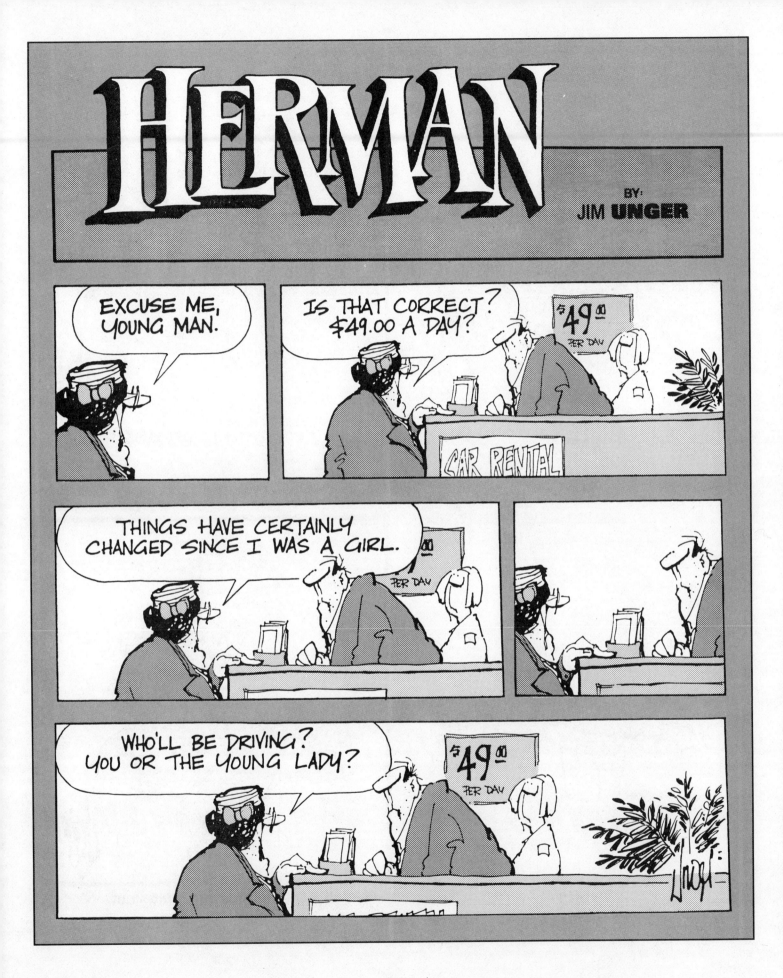

"They've given you two more years
for good behavior."

"Hand over your pacemaker."

"The honeymoon suite just
became available."

"One owner."

"I suppose you know you've been standing there for over an hour and the toaster's not plugged in."

"This won't help your back, but it makes me feel great."

"And the lucky winner is . . . No. 2."

"You'll have power steering if your wife drives."

"My heart nearly stopped. I thought I was looking in a mirror."

"We just want hot wax."

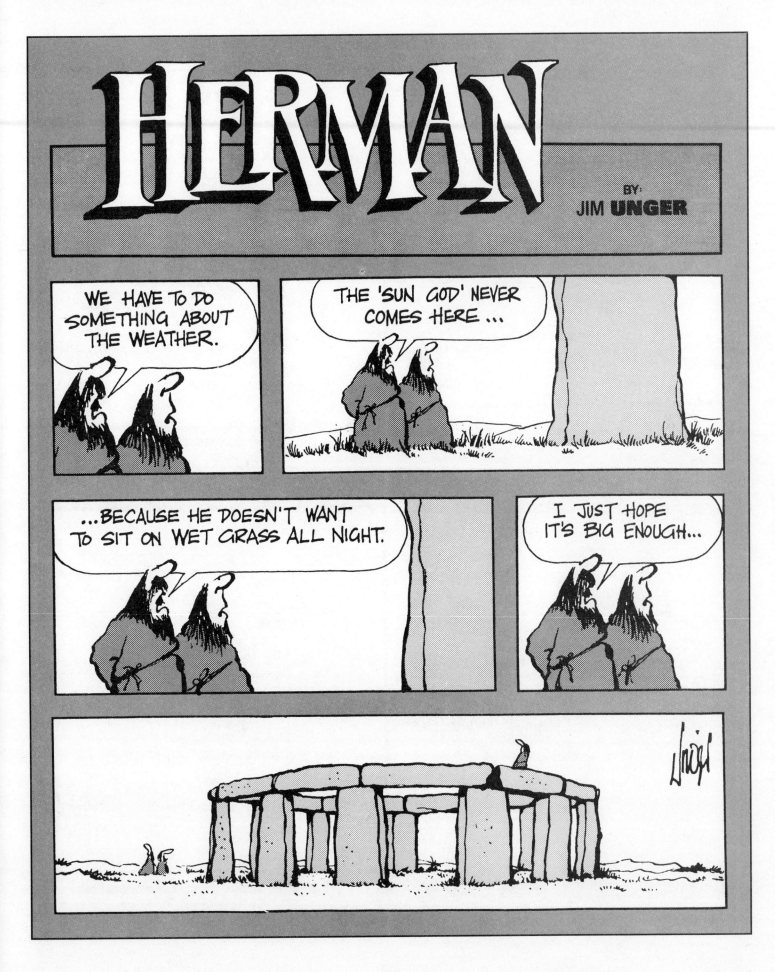

"Tell 'im."

"Just keep going left. If I'm not here when you get back, ask someone else."

"It states quite clearly . . . 'evening dress.'"

"With this $365 ring, plus sales tax, I thee wed."

"He's an exchange student."

"It's your little friend again, dear. He wants to borrow a 'dip' of sugar."

"It says here, 'Eat before last summer.'"

"Table for one near someone having sausages."

"One cola, no ice."

"Where do you want the decimal point?"

"Would I have worn this hat if
I was gonna smuggle?"

"Just how fast were you driving?"

"That's not the catch of the day, is it?"

"The doctor said to walk on it as much as possible."

"My candidate is determined to slash spending."

"I think I'll wear it like this. Then you won't have to keep reminding me how much it cost."

"Got a large table for six?"

"We're sharing the apartment. He gets it Mondays, Wednesdays, and Fridays."

"It's not even on the map."

"If this is 2 percent milk, how much am I paying for the other 98 percent?"

"I said, 'Is the in-season fruit *this* season or *next* season?'"

"Are these cornflakes biodegradable?"

"It's not my fault you're stupid."

"Pin these up in the kitchen and we won't have any mistakes."

"Oh yeah? Well, I just may not be
there when *you* get home!"

"And, of course, this model does
have the folding bicycle."

"Next time we'll get a taller plumber."

"Bend your knees."

"I don't care if it does work!
Put it back the way it was."

"Mildew, I know you like fruit, but you're
supposed to test one apple and one grape."

"So anyway, we got a date with these
two French waitresses . . ."

"I'm a trusty."

"Tourist or not, sir, I shall need to see a valid fishing permit."

"Let me write you a check for the other 40 cents."

"The baptism was 3 o'clock. We were definitely ahead of the wedding."

"Don't get too close. Remember what happened at the zoo."

"I don't want a son-in-law who's
stupid enough to marry
my daughter."

"So how did you break your arm?"

"Did you have to hang the food
right above the tent?"

"Oh no! Freezer burn!"

"It's my first day. I thought this was the staff canteen."

"Is this the one that caused all the controversy?"

"You're eating too much sugar."

"Is there any truth to the rumor that you're thinking of retiring from the ring?"

"Take your sign out of the window."

"A picture's supposed to speak a thousand
words. I can think of only one."

"I've got only $86 and 37 cents.
Is that reasonable?"

"My wife blew up that one."

"What part of the home did you put in these homemade cookies?"

"The judge looked at that new evidence I dug up and gave you another eight years."

"That's just in case you drop him."

"This next one is called 'Boats,'
by my eldest boy, Derek."

"Get going. I want a dollar's worth
around the neighborhood."

"What does it convert into? A tree house?"

"The body fits him, but the neck's too tight."

"Do you want to leave your glasses on?"

"How much are these orange
and black ones?"

"He's only allowed in the kitchen."

"I want to make sure these arrive in order."

"Same time next week."

"My wife thinks I'm in the shower."

"I need a tow to Chestnut Drive,
Wilmont Avenue, and Hill Street."

"I've decided to take a personal interest
in your career. You're fired."

"I told you I'd be a few minutes late."

"My blankets keep sliding off."

"How much longer are you going
to be on that phone?"

"Go and find someplace to plug that in."

"What happened to the TV?"

"It was yesterday."

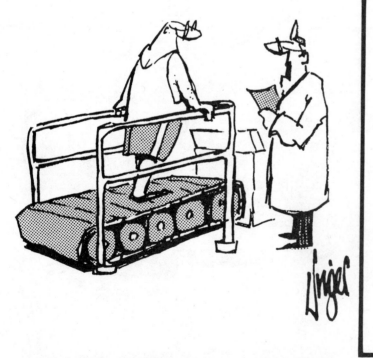

"What do you mean you're out of breath?"
I haven't switched it on yet!"

"My husband spent all weekend
trying to fix it."

"Sorry, pal, you can't come in here with a tie."

"You gonna be long? I'm double-parked."

"Take one of these out every four hours."

"Air bags for pedestrians."

"34 dollars and 50 cents."

"She had to come straight from work."

"I demand to know what you were doing in the kitchen at 3 o'clock in the morning."

"Do you think I'm pressing the
typewriter keys too hard?"

"Get lost."

"We bought another dog."

"Wait till you guys feel *this* leather."

114

"Found New Zealand yet, Benson?"

"I told you it wouldn't float."

"Only needs winding once a month."

"We don't have any!"

"Why are you looking in a book of gardening?"

"That's their new tamper-proof package."

"Nurse, where did we get those nitroglycerine tablets?"

"You knew it was today!"

"Thirty days or $350! If it's all the same to you, Judge, I'll take the money."

"I don't want my wife to find out I have an account here."

"The elevator's broken. I'll have to make several trips with all your luggage."

"Table for two near the band."

"Come on . . . it's not going to look like that on you."

"Two eighty-five? Here, take the $3 and drive another 100 yards."

"Now you've made his airbag go off."

"I didn't have any milk for your coffee so I put some white wine in it."

"All right, all right. Fifteen years less 37 minutes."

"Number 7."

"We were only out of the room for two minutes."

"One day, Damien, this will all belong to you. Three weeks later, it will all belong to the bank."

"Just a moment, sir."

"Tell Eddie I found his pen."

"You wanna look your best for the hospital."

"I'll get that adjusted."

"I recommend 8-ounce gloves
and protective headgear."

"Engagement rings."

"It wasn't your muffler."

"Want to see the wine list?"

"It's got a little camera on the front of it."

"It's just until I get my brakes fixed."

"You certainly don't have to pay for a large pepperoni if you only ordered a medium."

"You need a quart of oil and
a set of ovenproof dishes."

"You missed breakfast. It was
6 o'clock this morning."

"He's not a musician. That's
his new hearing aid."

"In a couple of days you should be well
enough to make it onto the chart."

"Just give them enough food for one."

"One of everything four times a day."

"It must have been in the bag of bananas."

"It's either your water pump or your stereo."

"I know it's a dog license! He was driving."

"Oh, boy! A world cruise."

"I hate the color but I'll take it."

"Which leg is it?"

"My kid drew them on my passport
picture with a Magic Marker."

"Caught any murderers lately?"

"I hear your wife had triplets."

"That's what you pointed at in the tank!"

"How do you expect me to average 55 miles an hour if I don't speed?"

"You can tell me now. I took the batteries out of his hearing aid."

"The toes are pinching."

"Is my prescription ready?"

"My wife threw my dinner at the wall and I framed it."

"I think I got most of it."

"Joyce, how do you spell 'juggling'?"

"Yeah, this feels about right."

"It's got a lovely view of the beach."

"I gotta be at the airport in 3 minutes. I'm driving."

"What's it going to be, food or college?"

"Where do you want me to wait?"

"How long does it take for a lottery ticket to dissolve in stomach acid?"

"I thought that was the exit."

"We've come to repossess your land."

"I'll just have a cup of coffee."

"I'm scared of heights."

"I'm not stealing it. I'm moving it closer to my house."

"I am *still* waiting for my change!"

"He had to give up the shoe-repair business."

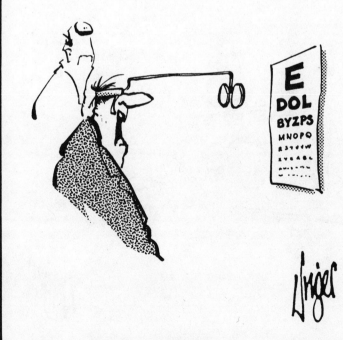

"Perfect!"

"I feel better when I can hear it."

"Want the inside done?"

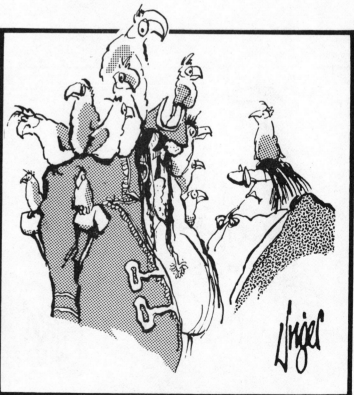

"His family flew in for a visit."

"E, C A B Z, M . . ."

"He said I could have breakfast
in bed every morning."

"I like a man with determination."

"I can see my filing cabinet."

"Now then, is that *blue* or *glue*?"

"You look like an endangered species."

"That guy in the red doesn't have any!"

"Sorry pal, we're right out of aircraft carriers."

"Can you spare a twenty?"

"Is that one owner since new
or one owner now?"

"Oh, no! Not your new golf shoes!"

"I put these on the ones I haven't done yet."

"The doctor said sleep on your stomach tonight and he'll see you first thing tomorrow."

"Taxi!"

"Next."

"Make up your stupid mind. Do you want me to cut your hair or not?"

"This is the only one we have in your size."

"Got a toothbrush with an extra-long handle?"

"What can you recommend for my wife? Apart from the obvious."

"196, 197, 198, 199 . . ."

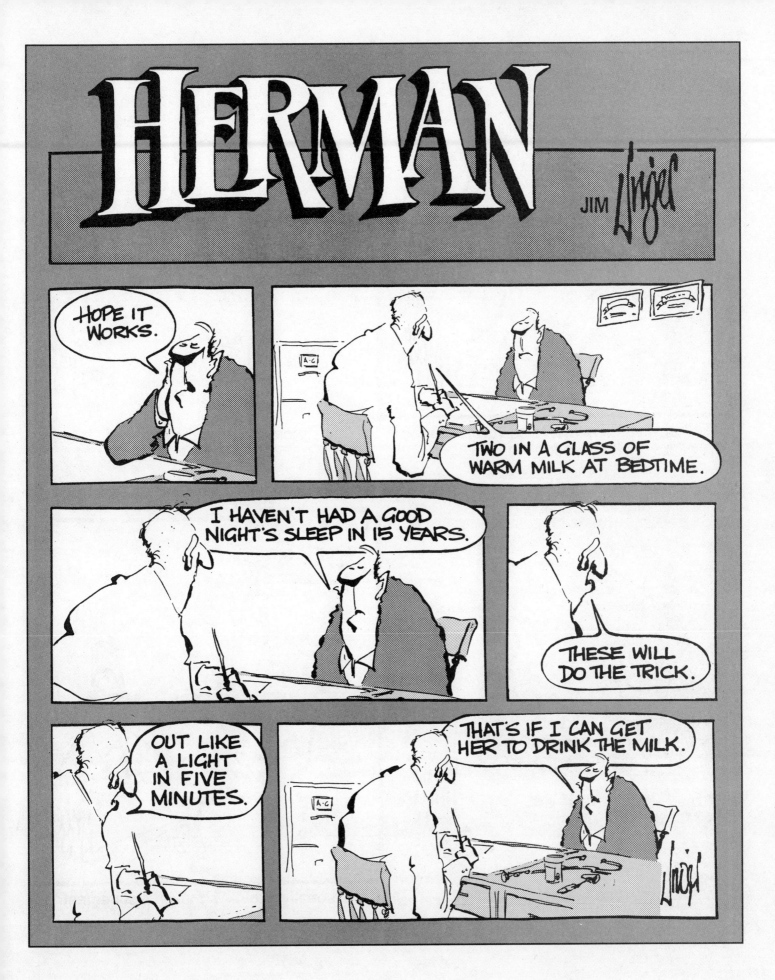

"Don't look at me. I told you to read the instruction manual."

"No charge for the sun roof."

"I reserved two stools for 7:30."

"Personally, I think it 'makes a statement.'"

"I *told* you not to use a rowing machine."

"I'm gonna use my car."

"I hear you're looking for someone who
can work without supervision."

"Twenty-eight percent of the rain
forest is now furniture."

"I'm increasing my odds."

"I had to get her $250,000 in
liability insurance."

"I'm going to have the buffet. Do you have
another one for my husband?"

"You need a second fitting."

"My hands are not as steady as they used to be."

"You said I could bring it back if my wife didn't like it."

"I found another one of these in his toolbox."

"I can't focus these binoculars."

PUBLIC LIBRARY

"I need another 3 1/2 inches."

"Three-piece set in elephant."

"Yes, yes, I know it's the other way!
I'm going around the world."

"I've got her finger size in this peanut butter."

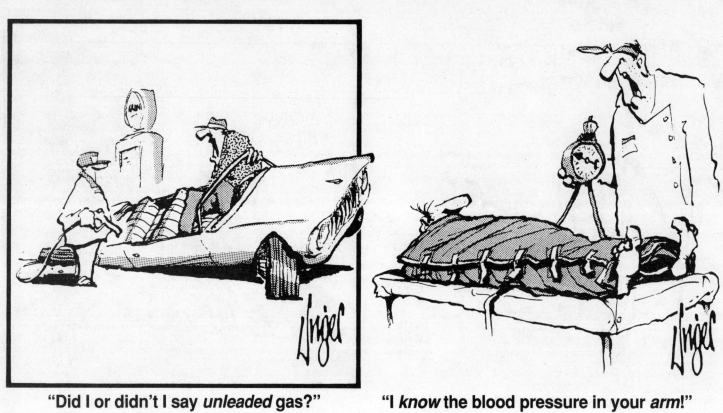

"Did I or didn't I say *unleaded* gas?"

"I *know* the blood pressure in your *arm*!"

"You can go ahead of me if
you're making a deposit."

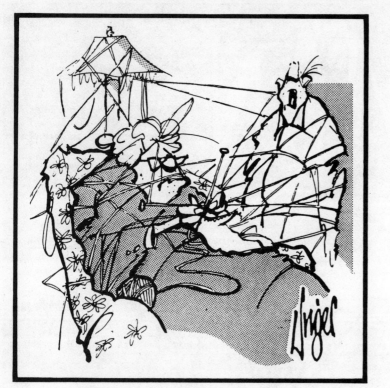

"Want me to put the cat out?"

"Our figures show that the larger lamps
are 68 percent less likely to
be stolen by burglars."

"Got a bigger mug?"

"Not one of his better works. But my dealer tells me it's the only one the artist ever painted upside down."

"I'll sign my brother-in-law's name till I get my memory back."

"For the man in a hurry."

"I'm not having you fall asleep at the wheel."

"How long before the snake comes out?"

"And it's about time they fixed up the rotten canteen in this place!"

"I can't say enough about this car."

"I asked my new secretary to get
me a sheet of graph paper."

"Keep talking. I'm just going to take a nap."

"No chain-smoking."

"You're still mounting the sidewalk on turns."

"The idiot couldn't find his cigarette lighter this morning."

"They never get enough sun at my place."

"It's our 'pre-Christmas giveaway.'"

"I always welcome new neighbors with one of my gooseberry pies . . . nine dollars."

"Walk on the inside. That's the tenth time
a cab has pulled over."

"OK, turn on your left side and
face the window."

"HE SAID, IT'S ALL YOUR FAULT."

"If you're calling about the night watchman position, it's gone."

"Hey! How many of these sticks equals two tablespoons?"

"Not so much ice next time."

"'Steven Edward' if it's a boy, 'Janet Annalise' if it's a girl."

"He said he saw his suitcase
fly past the window."

"The next six months will be mainly sunny
or cloudy, with dry and rainy spells.
Winds will be from most directions."

"Got any non-dairy creamer?"

"Gimme 15 seconds' worth of premium."

"I burned my arm. Your sausages
are under the stove."

"I thought so! He's gonna have to come through the window."

"Your room's upstairs. The ladder's in the garage."

"Want a bow on it?"

"There's a fly in my straw."

"Where do you want your
rosebushes planted?"

"Haven't you got any bigger tables?"

"I can only give you a few minutes."

"OK, OK, that's enough!"

173

"I'll just pay you when I'm sure I like it."

"It missed my new hat by that much."

"He must have remembered
your banana cake."

"What am I going to do if it rains?"

"They didn't have an 18-inch TV in stock so we had to take two nines."

"Waterproof up to 60 fathoms."

"Your interest starts *now*."

"I'd like to introduce you to my second wife, but I'm still stuck with the first one."

"Get ready, Mildred. After the green truck."

"We found your knees."

"My wife needs it for target practice."

"Got a pedal for a '91 Batmobile?"

"He was playing the violin."

"Six eggs, a jar of pickles, and
a packet of crackers."

"Good runner."

"I'll have to go and get my
toolbox from the car."

"I don't suppose you got the license
plate number, did you?"

"Joyce, ask Mr. Dennison if he's heard
of a composer named Mozart."

"We named him 'Uncle' after my mom's brother."

"Whaddya mean, '$1,000 a mile'?"

"I think he's starting to like that one."

"Pull!"

"It's Happy Hour. Do you want grape or raspberry?"

"Just the one suitcase."

"Joyce, what was that thing you bought for your car when it wouldn't start?"

"As soon as he starts snoring, slap it on."

"I strongly recommend the only thing we've got left."

"What have you got that's suitable for a three-year-old? It's my husband's birthday."

"After the commercial break, we'll talk to a woman who has spent her entire life making people miserable."

"For a man with $38 in the bank, you sure spend a lot of time reading the financial page."

"Mrs. Parker, most of this mail is for you."

"Your medical insurance has run out. You'll have to remove your own bandages."

"Quick, get a rope. Your brother Reggie's at the front door."

"How's he sleeping at night?"

"She needs a pair of backseat driving glasses."

"I'll have to adjust the brushes."

"Can my wife borrow your snow shovel?"

"Can I borrow your hedge trimmers for 18 years?"

"D'you want gravy on the jelly donut?"

"I'm perfectly capable of washing my face, Harold."

"Don't tell me this is hurting you more than it's hurting me."

"He's trying to remember what it used to be like before he started to work."

"I'll pass on the top letter and come back to it."

"All the people who had the 'fish spaghetti' for lunch want to check out."

"That was my mother on the phone. She said she hopes you're feeling worse."

"You say your lawyer bandaged your wrist?"

"Have you got any that just drop dead?"

"I take it you have the very best
medical insurance."

"I heard you say, 'There's some
old bat waiting'!"

Other Popular Herman Books